D1757324

Ramen for Beginners & Pros

The Cookbook with Japanese Noodle Recipes for Every Day

1st Edition

ISBN- 9781792810800

Table of contents

Introduction

A new trend is sweeping the land, a food trend that seems to stand against the Clean Eating ideology. Anything but vegan, the ramen soups from Japan are coming to Europe and continue the hype about bone broth from grandma's times. For the first time a Japanese dish that is not sushi is gaining ground in Europe. Ramen are a specific kind of Japanese noodles. Traditional Japanese soups that were made with these noodles were also called ramen. They capture us with an umami taste explosion while the vegan Clean Eating trend is trying to tell us that it is possible to do without strong flavors and spices. And yet, the two trends are not necessarily in conflict with each other. Food can be pleasantly intensely flavored and still vegan and healthy. Thus it happens sometimes that European restauranteurs make the original ramen soup without any meat or fish and use ready-made sauces to mix seasoning sauces instead of long fermentation processes. Nonetheless, we are trying to stick close to the original in this book and find a compromise between the hearty Japanese broth and the European palate.

We will teach you the art of preparing this particular soup in this book. The beauty of the ramen culture is that there are no dogmatic recipes that you need to follow exactly. It is more of a variable modular system. You will learn different basic recipes that you can combine as you wish or following some recommendations in this cookbook so that you will ultimately have your home-made ramen soup that you can enjoy. Most of the time, you prepare a basic broth first, then refine it with a sauce or some sort of seasoning broth and finally, as a third component there will be soup additions, so called toppings. The finished soup is usually named after the base broth that is used. Basically to differentiate here are Miso, Tonkutso, Shoyu and Shio. Miso soups are known for their strong fermented soy paste taste. Tonkutso is the meat or bone broth from Japan. Shoyu ramen are mostly based on the flavor of soy sauce and Shio is the seafood soup, which tastes salty and is made from fish and seafood. In reality, every ramen chef swears by their own secret recipe. Become one of those chefs yourself. You just need a certain fondness of experimenting. Take the recipes in this book and use them as inspiration to begin your own ramen journey.

Ramen soups are often known as instant dishes in Europe. Because they are full with flavor enhancers and other additives they gained a bad reputation in the health-conscious part of the population. Which might be justified for the instant soups. But those who associate ramen with poor nutrition have never enjoyed a real ramen soup that has been home-made with fresh ingredients. The soups give us insight into centuries-old recipes and methods of the Japanese kitchen. In this cookbook you will learn things about the traditional way of fermentation that is for example used for the production of soy sauce or miso paste. Without this complex process those products would never have reached Europe. Furthermore, old techniques are currently experiencing a sort of Renaissance and are taught here because of that.

Many don't know that the ramen soup did not originally come from Japan but from China. In the 19th century they came to the island and became known there and were perfected. While in China ramen was thought of as a traditional noodle soup with ingredients that were not closely defined, the modular composition as well as the characteristic taste of the soup developed in Japan. There, ramen is a hearty dish with a high fat content that is out of the question for our European taste buds. Because of that, the recipe ideas in this cookbook are not as fatty as the original, which does not mean that the classic pork broth will be ignored.

Besides the unfamiliar taste experience, there are other particular customs when eating ramen. In Japan biting the noodles means bad luck. Because of that the soup is slurped in its land of origin. When going to a ramen bar in a German-speaking area you will very rarely hear the slurping noise. Europeans have different table manners. In Japan it is also said that you should eat ramen as quickly as possible since the noodles taste best when hot. In some bars speaking while eating is forbidden to speed up the eating. This custom would also be hard to enforce in Europe.

Basics

Pork Broth Base

Ingredients:

800 g pork belly

6 chicken drumsticks

1 bunch mirepoix

1 garlic clove

100 g ginger

20 g kombu

Preparation:

1
Cut into pork belly horizontally and roll up. Tie together with yarn.

2
Wash drumsticks and mirepoix. Peel and cube the vegetables. Peel garlic clove and cut in half.

3
Peel and chop up the ginger. Put all ingredients in pot with 3 liters of water and bring to a boil.

4
Boil for 2 hours and regularly skim the foam off. After 1 ½ hours wipe off the kombu and add.

5   Take meat out and strain soup through a cloth.

6   Never add seasoning! That will be done with specific sauces or seasoning broths in the ramen dishes.

Dashi Broth

Time: 30 minutes | Four servings

Ingredients:

1 L water

10 g kombu alga

20 g bonito flakes

30 g niboshi (dried sardines)

2 dried shiitake mushrooms

Preparation:

1

Chop mushrooms and kombu. Soak mushrooms in water till they are fully expanded. Remove heads and middle of the niboshi. Add kombu alga and niboshi to the mushrooms and slowly bring to a boil.

2

Take out the kombu and niboshi, add dash of cold water and bonito flakes.

3

Bring to a boil again carefully and remove from heat to let it cool down slightly.

4

Strain broth. Depending on additions to soup, mushrooms can be added again.

Soy-Bonito Seasoning Broth

Ingredients:

1/8 L soy sauce

25 g bonito flakes

800 g cooked pork belly roll

Preparation:

1
  Bring half a liter water and soy sauce to a boil. Add bonito flakes and simmer for 20 minutes.

2
  Remove from heat and let cooked pork belly roll sit in the seasoning broth for one hour.

3
  Remove pork after one hour and strain seasoning broth through cloth.

Soy Sauce

Time: 6 to 12 months | Recipe makes four liters of soy sauce

Ingredients:

4 cups soy beans

water

4 cups flour

Koji starter

3.5 cups salt

Preparation:

1
Remove soy beans from shells and rinse in colander. Remove discolored beans. Soak beans overnight. You'll need approximately 5 liters of water for that.

2
Remove beans the next day and rinse. Cover beans with new water and cook for 4 to 5 hours till soft.

3
Mash cooked soy beans. Add flour and mix well till paste or dough forms. Let paste cool slightly and add the koji starter according to package instructions and mix well.

4   Put koji mix in casserole dish or something similarly low and wide. The mix should be no more than 5 cm high. Make 5 cm deep grooves using a finger or wooden spoon, similar to planting grooves in a vegetable garden, five to seven centimeters apart.

5   Let ferment for two days in a warm and damp place (e.g. kitchen: on top of the fridge or cupboard). The bacteria grow in a green color.

6   After two days, dissolve 3.5 cups salt in 3.8 L water. Add koji mix to the salt brine. Now it's called moromi. Put the moromi in a jar that holds at least seven liters and stir every day for the first week. For the next six to twelve months stir weekly.

7   Once the desired strength of flavor is reached, strain moromi through cloth. Squeeze cloth so that no liquid is lost. Discard solids. Heat liquid to 80°C and keep at that temperature for 20 minutes. Bottle after the pasteurization and store cool. The soy sauce keeps closed for up to three years.

Clear Chicken Broth

Ingredients:

Whole chicken or soup hen (1.5 kg) – 1

Water – 5 L

Onion – 2

Salt – to taste

Peppercorns – 1 tsp.

Preparation:

1

Put chicken or soup hen in large pot that holds 6 liters.

2

Add water to pot to cover meat completely. Bring to a boil over low heat. Skim off the foam and let cook covered for 5 to 6 hours. Peel onion, chop and add. Season with salt and pepper.

3

Remove meat (which you can use later for the topping!). Strain through colander and refrigerate till you use it.

Red Curry Paste

Time: 30 minutes | Recipe makes 200 ml curry paste

Ingredients:

7 chili peppers

2 onions

4 garlic cloves

2 sticks lemongrass

2 kaffir lime leaves

20 g ginger

1 Tbsp. coriander

1 Tbsp. cumin

1 Tbsp. miso paste

2 Tbsp. palm oil

1 Tbsp. salt

Preparation:

1
    Wash chilies, cut in half and remove seeds. Blanch chili halves in salt water for one minute. Peel and chop onions and garlic.

2
    Wash lemongrass and kaffir lime leaves and chop together with blanched chilies and ginger. If the spices are not ground, pound in mortar.

3
    Add all prepared ingredients with the miso paste, palm oil and salt to a heavy-duty mixer and mix. Alternatively, pound all ingredients to paste in mortar.

Garlic Paste

Ingredients:

Garlic heads (fresh) – 6

Sea salt – 200 g

Sesame oil – 1 Tbsp.

Canola oil – 1 Tbsp.

Dry white wine – 2 Tbsp.

Soy sauce - 1 Tbsp.

Preparation:

1 Heat oven to 160 degrees Celsius. Spread salt evenly on baking sheet.

2 Take heads of garlic apart and put on tray. Spread with sesame oil and bake for 30 minutes till soft.

3 Let garlic cool and then peel and chop. Add pieces along with white wine and soy sauce to tall mixing bowl and puree with mixer or emersion blender. While mixing, slowly add canola oil till solid paste forms.

4

Put garlic paste in a clean jar. For better preservation top the paste with a little bit of canola oil.

Miso Paste from Chickpeas

Time: 1 year

Ingredients:

900 g white rice

6 L spring water

1 g Koji starter

2 Tbsp. rice flour

800 g chickpeas

350 g non-iodized salt

Preparation:

1
Wash rice and let soak in water overnight.

2
Rinse rice next day and cook in fresh water. Knead in koji starter with rice flour. Cool rice to 35 °C or slightly cooler and then add starter. Spread rice on baking sheet, press down on it and cover with damp cloth. Let start for 40 hours in oven at 32 °C. Continuously dampen cloth to never let it dry out.

3
After 20 hours of aging, knead rice again and press it down again. If you notice discoloration in it, remove it immediately. Soak chickpeas in water overnight.

4   Rinse chickpeas the next day and cook in fresh water till soft. Regularly skim off foam and shells. As soon as the chickpeas are soft enough to crush between two fingers, remove them, saving the water. Mush a small portion of the chickpeas with 200 g of the salt, using a food processor or mixer to from a thick mash. Keep adding more chickpeas and continue to mix. Add some of the cooking water with each addition of chickpeas.

5   Mix koji rice and chickpea mash. Rub fermentation pot with salt. Form miso paste into compact ball, add to fermentation pot and press it into it. Cover with salt. Cover with cloth or plastic wrap and weigh down with a stone. The fermentation process will take one year from then on.

6   Check on miso paste after one to two months. Remove mold if present, using gloves. Stir paste so that liquid is back in the mash and press down again, cover with salt, cover with cloth or plastic wrap and weigh down again.

Peanut Butter

Time: 30 minutes | Recipe makes 300 ml peanut butter

Ingredients:

230 g unsalted peanuts

1 pinch salt

3 Tbsp. peanut oil

Preparation:

1   Soak peanuts overnight.

2   Rinse and drain nuts the next day. Preheat oven to 100 °C. Dry peanuts for 5 to 10 minutes.

3   Let nuts cool and then add to heavy-duty mixer with salt and peanut oil. Depending on desired consistency the peanut butter can be crunchy or creamy.

4   The peanut butter is slightly more liquid right after it's made then it will be later. It will keep for six weeks when stored in a cool place.

Tare Sauce

Time: 15 minutes

Ingredients:

2 cloves of garlic

1 thumb-big piece of ginger

2 green onions

3 Tbsp. honey

6 Tbsp. soy sauce

8 Tbsp. rice wine

2 Tbsp. sesame oil

Preparation:

1
Peel garlic. Slice ginger. Wash green onions and cut into rings. Chop all three up together.

2
Heat honey, soy sauce and rice wine in small pot while constantly stirring.

3
As soon as sauce is viscous add garlic, ginger, onions and sesame oil.

Ramen Noodles

Ingredients:

1 package baking powder

100 ml water

1 knife tip salt

200 g flour

Corn starch

Preparation:

1
    Preheat oven at 130 °C. Put parchment paper on baking sheet and spread with baking powder. Bake for one hour. Let cool without touching it, put baking powder in a jar.

2
    Mix 2 Tbsp. of the prepared baking powder with water.

3
    Mix water and salt with flour to for a dough. Knead for five minutes. The dough should sort of stick together. Wrap in plastic wrap and let rest for 15 minutes at room temperature.

4
    Knead again for five minutes. Roll out dough in between, fold and kneed some more. Wrap in plastic wrap and let rest for one hour.

5 Roll out dough 1 mm thin. It's easiest if you use a pasta machine for this and the next step. Use spaghetti attachment or cut 1 mm strips.

6 Divide noodles into four portions and form into a nest each. Sprinkle with corn starch. Dry in oven at low temperature or use immediately.

Soba Noodles

Time: 40 minutes | One serving

Ingredients:

100 g buckwheat

50 ml water

Preparation:

1
    Grind buckwheat and put through sieve. Discard edge layers.

2
    Knead flour and water into a solid dough and wrap in plastic wrap and let rest for 10 minutes.

3
    Divide dough in halves after letting it rest. Wrap one half in plastic wrap again.

4
    Press other half flat, roll out between two layers of parchment paper and fold ones each from top, bottom, left and right. Wrap the square in the parchment paper – fold the parchment paper on all four sides backwards. Roll out dough again so that it fills the square pocket of the parchment paper exactly. Unwrap the dough and roll out to the desired size. Then wrap it back up in the parchment paper and roll out the dough to fit the whole square again.

5   Wrap the rolled out dough in plastic wrap and repeat step 4 with the rest of the dough.

6   Cut both dough squares into thin strips, one at a time. The soba noodles can be cooked in salt water right away.

Naruto Maki – Japanese Fish pastry

Time: 2 hours | Four servings

Ingredients:

80 g beets

450 g swai or catfish

Ice-cold water

5 Tbsp. rice wine

Rice vinegar

10 g corn starch

12 g salt

15 g rice flour

1 Tbsp. soy sauce

Preparation:

1   Peel, dice and cook beets. Cut up cold fish filet and put into a heavy-duty mixer, along with 100 ml ice-cold water.

2   Add rice wine and rice vinegar and mix. Stir in corn starch, salt and 10 g rice flour and let dough rest for half an hour.

3   Drain beets, rinse under ice-cold water and let cool. Preheat oven to 110 °C. Grease a piece of aluminum foil with butter and spread two thirds of the dough onto it using a wide knife that you rinsed under cold water. Puree beets and stir into the remaining dough, along with the soy sauce and 5 g rice flour.

4   Spread the colorful mix onto the fish dough and roll up with the help of the foil. Pull the foil up to do so.

5   Place a bowl of water in the bottom of the oven and place the fish roll on top of the aluminum foil in a casserole dish onto a rack above that. Reduce the temperature to 100 °C and steam for one hour.

6   After that you can easily cut the fish roll into slices and use as a soup topping.

Chashu

Ingredients:

450 g pork shoulder

2 garlic cloves

4 cm ginger root

2 green onions

2 Tbsp. clarified butter

150 ml soy sauce

100 ml rice wine

2 Tbsp. maple syrup

8 peppercorns

Preparation:

1 Cut meat horizontally, roll up and tie up with yarn. Peel garlic and cut ginger into slices.

2 Cut green onions in half the long way. Heat clarified butter in pot and sauté pork in it.

3 Take meat out and heat up soy sauce, rice wine, maple syrup and peppercorns together. Add prepared ingredients as soon as the liquid begins to boil.

4 Cover meat with water and stew covered for one to one and a half hours. Turn meat over every 15 minutes. Chashu can be used as a soup topping or something else. The broth can be used as a base for soup or to make menma.

Menma

Ingredients:

50 g dried bamboo strips

150 ml chashu broth

150 ml water

2 Tbsp. chili oil

Preparation:

1
Soak dried bamboo for at least six hours, changing the water every two hours.

2
After that, gently squeeze bamboo strips and cook in a chashu broth and water mix.

3
The liquid mix should follow the amount in the recipe and have a 1:1 proportion and be seasoned with chili oil.

4

The bamboo strips should be cooked for 45 minutes on low heat, so that they don't burn. Stir frequently. After 45 minutes most of the liquid should be cooked off.

Kamaboko – Fish Paste from Salmon

Ingredients:

250 g salmon filet

60 ml water

7 g salt

16 g flour

7 g corn starch

2 Tbsp. rice wine

Preparation:

1
Cut up salmon filet and soak in ice-cold water. Dry after a few minutes with a cloth and finely chop using a mortar, food processor or heady-duty mixer.

2
Add a little bit of ice-cold water at a time during the processing till a total of 60 ml are used up.

3
Add salt, flour, corn starch and rice wine and continue to process it and then form into a half roll. Now let mixture rest for one hour.

4

After letting it rest, steam for half an hour, then let cool. Kamaboko is used as a soup topping or can be fried and served as a side.

Ramen Egg

Time: 15 minutes | Two servings

Ingredients:

2 Tbsp. soy sauce

2 Tbsp. rice wine

water

2 eggs

Preparation:

1
Mix soy sauce, rice wine and water in a tightly sealable container.

2
Boil water in a little pot and carefully add the two eggs. Reduce heat and cook eggs for six minutes, rinse under cold water and peel carefully.

3
Add eggs to the container, making sure they are completely covered with marinade. Marinate for at least four hours, best wait till the next day. The eggs are cut in half and used as a soup topping.

Chashu (Marinated, Stewed Pork)

Time: approx. 20 minutes + time to cook

Ingredients:

Garlic cloves – 4-5

Ginger (thumb-big) – 1 piece

Shallots – 2

Green onion – 1 bunch

Pork collar – 500 g

Frying oil – 2 Tbsp.

Dark soy sauce – 175 ml

Sake – 120 ml

Mirin – 60 ml

Cane sugar – 75 g

Preparation:

1 Peel and chop garlic. Peel ginger and shallots and slice thinly. Thinly slice green onions.

2 Tie pork collar with kitchen yarn and place in ovenware. Heat oil in the pot and sear meat on all sides until it is very tender.

3 Mix together other ingredients (ginger, shallots, garlic, green onions, soy sauce, sake, mirin and cane sugar) and pour over the meat and add

enough boiling water to cover the meat completely. Stew for 3-4 hours at low temperature (rotate meat regularly!).

4

Take finished chashu out of the pot and cut thin strips off of it when desired.

Marinated Tofu

Time: active time: approx. 15 minutes, resting time: approx. 25-45 minutes

Ingredients:

Tofu (plain, firm) – 300 g

Medium cloves of garlic – 3

Ginger (3 to 4 cm) – 1 piece

Paprika – 1 tsp.

Sugar – 1 tsp.

Soy sauce – 4 Tbsp.

Oil for frying

Chili pepper – 1

Salt and pepper – to taste

Preparation:

1

Cut tofu in approx. 1 cm thin slices. To press liquid out of tofu, place heavy book or board on tofu for about 10 minutes. After that, dry with paper towel or wrap in one.

2

Peel garlic and ginger and grate it or alternatively dice very finely. Place garlic and ginger in a bowl, add soy sauce, paprika and sugar and mix to make a marinade.

3

Have a flat bowl ready with a side that is slightly taller than the tofu pieces. Place half of the marinade in the bowl. Place tofu pieces next to each other in the marinade and pour the rest of the marinade evenly over the slices.

4

Marinate for 15-30 minutes, turn slices over ones and let marinate for another 10-15 minutes. As soon as the tofu absorbs the marinade it turns a dark color.

5

Fry tofu slices in oil over low to medium heat on all sides. Add salt, pepper or coarsely chopped chili to taste.

Tip: When you remove the liquid from the plain tofu it can soak up the marinade much better. Additionally, it can be fried better and gets crispier! When marinating you should also not use oil, since that coats the tofu and does not let the marinade soak in as easily.

Ramen Soup Dishes

Simple Ramen Soup

Ingredients:

Sesame

500 g ramen noodles

Salt

4 eggs

3 green onions

1 ringed beet

800 g cooked pork belly

3 L basic broth

½ L seasoning broth

cress

Preparation:

1

Soak sesame the night before.

2

Prepare noodles according to package instructions the next day. Soft-boil eggs for six minutes.

3

Wash green onions and cut into rings. Peel ringed beet and slice very thinly.

4   Rinse eggs under cold water. Peel and cut in half.

5   Cut up cooked meat. Rinse noodles under cold water. Divide toppings
        in seven bowls. Mix basic broth and seasoning broth and poor over it.

6   Rinse sesame. Garnish ramen soup with cress and sesame.

Shio-Ramen Classic

Time: approx. 20 minutes | Servings: 2

Ingredients:

Canned corn – 125 g

Green onion – 1

Chicken broth – 800 ml

Salt - 1 tsp.

Dried ramen noodles – 100 g

Carrots – 2

Bamboo sprouts – 60 g

Nori strips (7 x 4 cm) – 2

Narutomaki – 2 slices

Sesame – to taste

Oil for frying

Preparation:

1   Add corn and 2 Tbsp. oil in a pan and fry the corn over medium heat. Clean green onion and slice into thin rings.

2   Heat chicken broth in soup pot over medium heat till it is almost boiling. Just before it's boiling, add salt, turn heat off, mix well and let sit for 2 minutes.

3   At the same time: Bring 1 liter water to a boil in a different pot, add ramen noodles and cook according to packaging to al dente. Then drain in colander and let drain well (do not rinse with water!)

4   Julienne carrots.

5   To serve divide chicken broth in two bowls, add noodles and garnish with narutomaki slices, green onions, carrots, bamboo sprouts, corn, nori and sesame.

Tip: Fresh bamboo sprouts always have to be cooked! Raw they contain a poisonous hydrocyanic acid glycoside, which is rendered harmless when heated!

Shio-Ramen with Chashu and Curry

Time: 30 Minutes | Servings: 2

Ingredients:

Egg – 1

Mushrooms – 200 g

Green onion – 1

Ginger (2 cm) – 1

Garlic glove – 1

Onion – 1

Curry powder – 1½ Tbsp.

Flour – 1½ Tbsp.

Pepper – 1 knife tip

Chicken broth – 800 ml

Dried ramen noodles – 100 g

Chili oil – 2 Tbsp.

Chashu – 2-4 slices

Sesame seeds – to taste

Oil for frying

Preparation:

1   Soft boil egg, rinse under cold water, peel and cut in half. Clean mushrooms and cut in half.

2   Cut green onion in rings and put aside. Peel and chop ginger and garlic. Peel onion, chop and fry till transparent in pot with a little bit of oil over medium heat. After that, add ginger and garlic and fry for another minute.

3   Add curry powder, pepper and flour to the pot and cook at low temperature.

4   Slowly add 200 ml chicken broth to the pot (careful: hot steam!) and whisk well. Cook curry mix for another 5 minutes (till curry has slightly thickened).

5   Let the rest of the chicken broth simmer in a different pot over medium heat.

6   At the same time: cook ramen noodles in a separate pot according to package instructions till al dente. Drain in colander and shake well.

7

Divide curry mix in two soup bowls. Fill bowl with chicken broth and chili oil. To mix the curry mix with the broth and the oil, stir soup briefly with chop stick. Now add the noodles and garnish with chashu, egg, mushrooms, green onion rings and sesame seeds. DONE!

Shio-Ramen with Broccoli and Shrimp

Ingredients:

For the tare:

Ginger – 20 g

Dashi – 300 ml

Sake – 50 ml

Lime juice – 3 Tbsp.

Sea salt – to taste

For the dish:

Dried wakame alga (finely chopped) – 10-15 g

Small shrimp – 12-24

Oil – 2 Tbsp.

Salt – to taste

Green onions – 2

Fresh broccoli (alternatively: 1 package frozen broccoli) – ½ kg

Dried ramen noodles – 200 g

Vegetable broth – 600 ml

Additionally:

Wooden skewer – 12-24

Preparation:

1   For the tare: Peel ginger, grate finely, mix in a pot with sake, dashi and lime juice and briefly bring to a boil. To give the tare a definite salty taste, it is seasoned with sea salt.

2   For the dish: Put the wakame alga in a pot to soak and pour hot water over it. After 5 minutes, put in a colander and rinse well with cold water.

3   Peel shrimp to the last link. Cut open shrimp on the back and remove intestine. Then put shrimp on skewers.

4   Heat oil in pan. Fry shrimp skewers for 2-4 minutes on all sides until they are pink on the outside and still transparent on the inside. Salt.

5   Wash green onions, slice thinly and put aside to use as a topping. In a different pot, blanch broccoli for 1-2 minutes.

6   Cook ramen noodles according to package instructions in 1 L salt water till al dente. Drain in fine colander (shaking it back and forth to drain noodles well).

7

Heat vegetable broth and tare in separate pots. Pour boiling tare in 2 big soup bowls. Divide wakame alga and broccoli in the bowls and fill with boiling vegetable broth. Garnish soup with green onions and shrimp skewers.

Tonkotsu Ramen

Time: 3 – 4 hours | Servings: 6

Ingredients:

1 bunch mirepoix

1 head of garlic

100 g ginger

800 g pork belly

6 chicken wings

Water

20 g kombu

125 ml soy sauce

25 g bonito flakes

20 g snow peas

300 g carrots

Salt

2 Tbsp. red curry paste

2 Tbsp. coconut oil

500 g ramen noodles

Cress

Preparation:

1   Wash mirepoix, peel and dice. Peel garlic and cut in half.

2   Peel ginger and chop. Cook cut up ingredients together with the pork belly and the chicken wings in three liters of water for two hours. Add kombu after one and a half hours and cook.

3   Remove pork and pour off broth. Prepare seasoning broth from 750 ml water and soy sauce. Let bonito flakes simmer in it for 20 minutes. After that, let pork sit in it for one hour.

4   Wash snow peas and peel carrot. Cut both into strips. Bring three liters water and three teaspoons of salt to a boil for noodles.

5   Mix 4 tablespoons seasoning broth with curry paste. Cube meat and fry in coconut oil. Deglaze with curry mix. Pour off seasoning broth.

6   Boil noodles. Divide soup additions in bowls, mix basic broth with seasoning broth and pour over it. Garnish with cress.

Vegetarian Kotteri Ramen

Time: 90 minutes | Six servings

Ingredients:

2 bunches mirepoix

100 g ginger

1 head of garlic

3 L water

20 g kombu

4 baby bok choy

300 g shiitake mushrooms

500 g hokkaido pumpkin

300 g ramen noodles

4 eggs

Salt

3 Tbsp. coconut oil

5 tsp. miso paste

6 Tbsp. soy sauce

2 Tbsp. peanut butter

2 Tbsp. sambal oelek

cress

Preparation:

1

Wash, peel and dice mirepoix. Peel and chop ginger.

2

Peel garlic and cut in half. Add prepared ingredients to a pot with 3 liters water and heat up. Simmer for one hour.

3

Carefully wipe off kombu and add after 45 minutes.

4

Meanwhile, wash bok choy and mushrooms and cut in half. Wash pumpkin, cut in half, take the seeds out and cube.

5

Prepare noodles and eggs in salt water. Sauté mushrooms in coconut oil. Take them out and sauté pumpkin.

6

Heat 300 ml water with miso paste and soy sauce. Drain and keep vegetable broth, mix with seasoning broth and peanut butter as well as the sambal oelek. Rinse eggs under cold water, peel and cut in half.

7

Put noodles, pumpkin, bok choy, mushrooms and eggs in bowls and top with the broth. Garnish with cress.

Ramen Soup with Meatballs

Ingredients:

1 onion

400 g ground beef

1 egg

2 Tbsp. bread crumbs

2 Tbsp. soy sauce

Salt, pepper

1 zucchini squash

½ celery rib

1 L dashi broth

270 g ramen noodles

2 Tbsp. miso paste

Chives

Preparation:

1   Peel and chop onion. Salt and pepper ground beef, mix with egg, bread crumbs and soy sauce and form meatballs.

2   Wash zucchini and celery. Slice zucchini in thin strips and cut celery in slices.

3   Put water on for noodles. Heat broth and cook vegetables and meatballs in it for 10 minutes. Cook noodles.

4   Take out a ladle full of broth and mix miso paste into it. Then add back into broth.

5   Wash chives and chop. Drain noodles, rinse under water and divide into bowls. Pour broth over them and garnish with chives.

Miso Soup

Time: 30 minutes | Four servings

Ingredients:

160 g tofu

1 piece aburaage

½ leek

5 potatoes

1 handful soy bean sprouts

1 handful spinach

10 g wakame seaweed

750 ml dashi broth

60 g miso paste

Preparation:

1   Dice tofu. Chop aburaage. Wash leek and cut into rings. Peel and dice potatoes, parboil in a small pot.

2   Wash sprouts and spinach. Cut spinach into strips.

3   Let wakame seaweed soak for 5 minutes and then drain.

4   Bring dashi broth to a boil. Cook tofu, aburaage and wakame in it for 2 minutes.

5   Take soup off heat and stir miso paste into it.

6   Add leek, potatoes, sprouts and spinach.

Ramen from Tokyo

Time: 45 minutes | Four servings

Ingredients:

1 L dashi broth or other base broth

120 g (cooked) roast pork

2 garlic cloves

2 leeks

Ginger

Salt, pepper

Soy sauce

100 g spinach

2 eggs

500 g ramen noodles

225 g bean sprouts

Butter

80 g naruto maki (fish pastry)

3 g nori alga

Preparation:

1

Slowly heat up broth, if you use raw meat, cook in broth in one piece. Peel and chop garlic. Wash leek and cut into rings.

2

Chop ginger. Add garlic, leek and ginger to broth and season with salt, pepper and soy sauce.

3

Wash and blanch spinach. Boil eggs. Slice pork.

4

Prepare noodles. Wash sprouts and add to soup. Peel eggs and cut in half.

5

Drain noodles and rinse under cold water. Divide into bowl. Add a small piece of butter in the middle of each bowl. Put two slices of pork, a little bit of fish pastry, half an egg, a handful of spinach and nori alga in each bowl. Pour broth over it.

Soba-Soup with Pan-fried Beef

Ingredients:

300 g Beef

Coconut oil

100 g shiitake mushrooms

400 ml dashi broth

Soy sauce

1 pinch salt

2 green onions

3 Tbsp. cooking wine

500 g soba noodles

150 g spinach

Chili powder

Preparation:

1
Dice beef and fry on both sides in coconut oil. Wash mushrooms and slice.

2
Mix 300 ml dashi broth with half tablespoon soy sauce and salt. Simmer meat and mushrooms in seasoning broth for 5 minutes.

3
Wash green onions and cut into rings.

4
Heat cooking wine in pot. Once it starts to boil, add dashi broth. Once it starts to boil again, add 80 ml soy sauce.

5
Prepare noodles. Blanch spinach. Mix together broth and seasoning sauce.

6
Drain noodles, rinse under cold water and divide into soup bowls. Pour broth over them.

7
Add meat, spinach, green onion and mushrooms to the soup bowls and season with a pinch of chili powder.

Sumashijiru with Shrimp

Time: 30 - 45 minutes | Four servings

Ingredients:

750 ml dashi broth

1 tsp. soy sauce

Salt

4 carrots

1 tsp. rice wine

80 g shrimp

1 tsp. potato starch

½ leek

1 bunch ramp or ramson

chives

Preparation:

1   Bring dashi broth, soy sauce and 1 teaspoon salt to boil. Peel carrots, slice and boil in broth till soft.

2   Add pinch of salt to rice wine and add shrimp. Then roll in potato starch.

3   Blanch pre-cooked shrimp or cook raw shrimp in broth.

4   Wash leek and ramp. Cut leek into rings and ramp into strips and add both to the soup. Wash and chop chives.

5   Divide soup into bowls and garnish with chives.

Tonkutso-Ramen for the German Cuisine

Time: 20 minutes + 40 minutes | Four servings

Ingredients:

1 onion

3 garlic cloves

2 kg soup meat

1 Tbsp. honey

2 Tbsp. rice vinegar

2 Tbsp. white wine

5 Tbsp. soy sauce

Ginger

1 carrot

½ leek

1 celery rib

Pos. 1 broccoli stem or other cabbage stem

Parsley, lovage

500 g ramen noodles

4 eggs

1 handful spinach

2 green onions

2 Tbsp. mung bean sprouts

Preparation:

1

The night before, cut onion in half and with peel put into a pot. Peel garlic and press into pot. Cut meat off bone and add to pot with onion and garlic. Put meat aside for now. Pour 3 liters of water over it and boil.

2

Bring soup to a boil again the next day and add meat. Mix honey, rice vinegar, white wine and soy sauce in a small pot.

3

Grate ginger and add to seasoning broth. Remove meat from base broth and add to the small pot. Add enough broth to just cover the meat. Bring seasoning broth to a boil and then remove from heat immediately. Let sit.

4

Peel and cut carrot. Wash leek, celery and broccoli stem, if using. Cut leek and celery into rings. Wash and chop parsley and lovage. Cook vegetables and herbs in the base broth.

5

Prepare noodles. Hard-boil eggs. Put base broth through colander and mix with seasoning broth.

6

Wash spinach and green onions. Remove meat and vegetables from broth and cut spinach and green onions into strips and rings, respectively. Bring meat, cooked vegetables and green onions to a boil in the broth for one last time.

7

Drain noodles, rinse under cold water and divide in soup bowls. Rinse eggs under cold water, peel and cut into slices. Divide egg slices, sprouts and spinach in bowls and add broth, the rest of the vegetables and the meat.

Shoyu-Ramen with Chashu

Time: 40 minutes | Two servings

Ingredients:

1 cup chicken parts

1 egg

1 green onion

¼ nori alga

4 chashu slices

3 Tbsp. soy sauce

½ tsp. salt

2 Tbsp. rice wine

100 g ramen noodles

60 g bamboo sprouts

2 slices narutomaki

Pepper

Preparation:

1   Cook meat in 800 ml water. Boil egg in simmering water for 10 minutes.

2   Wash green onion and cut into rings. Cut nori in half and wrap chashu in it.

3   Rinse egg under cold water, peel and cut in half. Remove chicken pieces from chicken broth, heat the broth and season with soy sauce, salt and rice wine. Then remove from heat and let rest.

4   Meanwhile, prepare ramen noodles.

5   Divide broth into soup bowls. Add chashu, bean sprouts, narutomaki, half an egg and green onions. Then drain noodles and add and season to taste with pepper.

Snacks, Desserts and Other Ideas

Gyoza - Dumplings

Ingredients:

400 g wheat flour

340 ml water

2 pinch salt

1 napa cabbage

3 green onions

2 carrots

1 garlic clove

1 piece ginger

500 g ground beef

4 Tbsp. soy sauce

3 Tbsp. sesame oil

Clarified Butter

Preparation:

1

Knead flour, water and salt into a smooth dough. Cover with damp cloth and let rest for half an hour.

2

Wash cabbage and green onions and chop. Peel carrots and grate.

3

Peel and press garlic. Press ginger as well. Mix prepared ingredients with ground beef, soy sauce and sesame oil.

4

Roll out dough and use a 10 cm diameter cookie cutter to cut.

5

Put a tablespoon of the mix on top of each dough round and fold it in half. Press contact point together to make little folds.

6

Heat clarified butter in pan and place gyozas in it, close together, and fry. Fill pan with water to 2 cm height, cover and steam until water is gone.

Caramelized Spareribs

Time: 90 minutes | Four servings

Ingredients:

500 g spareribs

1 garlic clove

1 green onion

1 tsp. broth

½ tsp. salt

½ tsp. pepper

20 anchovy filets

8 Tbsp. soy sauce

1 tsp. clarified butter

1 tsp. honey

150 ml coconut water

Preparation:

1
Separate spareribs into single ribs and cut each bone in half, using poultry shears.

2
Peel and chop garlic. Wash and chop white part of green onion.

3
Mix broth, salt, pepper, garlic and green onion and marinate spareribs in it for 15 minutes.

4
Meanwhile, chop anchovies and mash with fork.

5
Then, mix with soy sauce to make a fish sauce.

6
After the waiting time is over, heat clarified butter in a pot and add honey. Once the honey begins to caramelize, add spareribs and sauté on high.

7
Add coconut water and 1 tsp of the fish sauce and let spareribs simmer covered for 20 minutes.

8

After cooking time is over, stir well and let simmer uncovered for another 20 minutes. Wash the green part of the green onion, chop and use to garnish the ribs.

Matcha-Almond-Ice Cream

Time: 5 hours | One serving

Ingredients:

50 g almonds

15 g matcha powder

100 g sugar

250 ml milk

250 ml cream

Preparation:

1

Soak almonds the day before.

2

Rinse almonds the next day, blanch, peel and drain. Put matcha powder and sugar in mixing bowl. Add a little bit of milk and beat with whisk to make a paste.

3

Add rest of milk and whisk. Whip cream and fold into matcha milk.

4

Grind up almonds and fold under.

5

Put mix into cold-resistant container and freeze for 5 hours. Stir the ice cream every half an hour during that time.

Mochi Ice Cream

Ingredients:

100 g sticky rice flour

2 Tbsp. sugar

¼ tsp. salt

110 ml water

Potato starch

Ice cream of choice

Preparation:

1

Mix sticky rice flour with sugar and salt. Add water and whisk until a homogenous mixture forms.

2

Place mixture into metal bowls and place into steam basket and steam for 15 minutes.

3

Spread potato starch on counter. After it's steamed, squeeze dough well using a spoon and pour onto counter. Sprinkle with starch and form into a roll.

4   Divide into six portions and knead each one, kneading some potato starch into it and press flat.

5   Place a teaspoon of ice cream as a filling on each dough disk and roll into ball. You have to work fast, since the dough gets tough when it gets cold.

Ramen Carbonara

Time: 30 minutes | One serving

Ingredients:

1 egg

1 egg yolk

50 g parmesan

2 bacon strips

200 g ramen noodles

2 Tbsp. coconut oil

Salt, pepper, soy sauce

1 green onion

Preparation:

1

Grate parmesan and mix 30 g of it with egg, egg yolk and pepper.

2

Prepare ramen noodles. Wash green onion and cut into rings. Cut bacon into strips and fry in coconut oil, together with green onion.

3

Add a little bit of noodle water to the bacon. Once noodles are done, add to pan. Take pan off heat and mix egg mixture into it.

4   If necessary, add more noodle water. Season sauce with salt and
pepper. Garnish on plates with parmesan.

Ramen Burger

Time: 30 minutes | Two servings

Ingredients:

400 g ramen noodles

1 egg

Coconut oil

2 burger patties

Arugula

1 green onion

1 pickle

Teriyaki sauce

Preparation:

1

Prepare noodles, drain and mix with egg. Divide into four.

2

Heat coconut oil and fry each noodle portion separately, until noodles get hard and stick together. Then flip and fry on the other side.

3

Let ramen rolls drain on paper towels and fry burger patties. Wash arugula.

4   Wash green onion and cut into rings. Cut pickle into slices lengthwise.

5   Place all ingredients on two ramen rolls, drizzle with teriyaki sauce and cover with the other two ramen rolls.

Disclaimer

This book contains opinions and ideas of the author and is meant to teach the reader informative and helpful knowledge while being entertaining. The instructions and strategies are possibly not right for every reader and there is no guarantee that they work for everyone. Using this book and implementing the information / recipes therein contained is explicitly your own responsibility and risk. This work with all its contents, does not guarantee correctness, completion, quality or currentness of the provided information. Misinformation or misprints cannot be completely eliminated.

Legal notice

Kentaro Asano by proxy of:

c/o Bianca Kronsteiner

impressumservice.net

Robert-Preußler-Straße 13 / TOP 1

5020 Salzburg

AT – Österreich

dibookspace@gmail.com

Cover design / concept:

oliviaprodesign | fiverr.com

Cover images:

Blinovita Depositphotos

Printed in Great Britain
by Amazon